instant calm

KAREN
SALMANSOHN

instant
calm

2-MINUTE MEDITATIONS
TO CREATE A LIFETIME
OF HAPPY

TEN SPEED PRESS
California | New York

contents

acknowledgments

First, I'd love to say a humongous thank-you to Ari Salmansohn and Howard Schwartz—who make my heart smile every day.

Next up, I'd love to thank my amazing "soul-editor," Lisa Westmoreland—for always bringing out the best in me as a writer.

Plus many thanks to my awesome "agent entourage": Celeste Fine, Jaidree Braddix, Sarah Passick, and Anna Petkovich.

Oh, and I'd also love to share my appreciation for my delightfully talented designer Lisa Bieser and the beautifully gifted illustrator Sarah Ferone.

introduction

FOR MANY YEARS I had recurring issues with stress.

Being worried and overwhelmed regularly kept me feeling distracted, unproductive, and less emotionally connected to the people I loved. Just thinking about that time makes me want to reach back through a time tunnel and hug my past self!

Thankfully, there was one technique that truly helped me with my anxiety. Actually, this technique pretty much saved me—and still does.

It's a type of meditation that taps into the five senses: sight, sound, touch, taste, and smell. I love doing these sensory meditations—not only because they are fun, but also because they work incredibly effectively to calm my busy, chattering-monkey mind.

As soon as I developed the practice of using these sensory meditations, I started to feel more calm and confident—even when a challenge would strike.

Loving reminder: These suggestions are not meant to take the place of a health care provider. If you have physiological concerns or you feel your anxiety is truly troubling you, please check in with a professional.

These sensory meditations work in a powerful and quick way because they direct your attention to one of your specific senses. This mental refocusing then happily distracts your brain from your worries—and retrains your brain to focus instead on the peace of the present moment.

I'm not the only one who loves and recommends sensory meditations as a method for relaxation. So do psychologists, yogis, neuroscientists, and university researchers. Often referred to as *grounding tools*, *anchors*, *one-pointed meditations*, or *concentration meditations*, sensory meditations have been shown to offer many benefits. They can help

- relax the mind.
- encourage the mind to be more open to other choices and think in new ways.
- release the anxiety that might otherwise lead to stress-induced habits, like overeating and smoking.
- improve how quickly people learn.
- reset your brain and body to deal with anxiety from a place of inner strength and greater clarity—so that you stay calm and confident even in the midst of challenges.

- stop obsessive anxious thoughts.
- calm you quickly when you're dealing with uncomfortable feelings, like anger, fear, grief, or self-loathing.
- retrain your brain to focus better—which means you're more able to focus on solutions.

For all these reasons, meditation is regularly being prescribed by mainstream doctors as a tool to help patients combat stress, reduce high blood pressure, and even regulate hormone levels.

These days lots of doctors and psychiatrists are recognizing the amazing powers of meditation to calm people down—and make them feel more balanced.

- Harvard researchers have reported that mindfulness meditation can increase cortical thickness in the brain's hippocampus (the brain zone in charge of learning, memory, emotion regulation, and more). They also found that meditation reduces brain cell density in the amygdala (the region that helps trigger physical reactions to fear and anxiety, among other things).

Fun fact: Some people even think of hypnosis as a form of meditation. For example, hypnosis spirals and crystal pendulums each work because they focus your vision and mind in a concentrated way on an object. As a result, you stop paying attention to the chatter in your mind and enter into a deep state of relaxation.

- UCLA research has reported that meditation plumps up the gray matter volume throughout the brain, which can change your brain for the better, helping you to calm down and learn to focus more successfully during stressful times.

- A review of research at Johns Hopkins found that meditation seems to have as much effect as antidepressants when it comes to improving some symptoms of mild or moderate depression.

Unfortunately, a lot of people find meditation boring or hard to do. They complain that they feel restless and uneasy attempting to sit, be still, and meditate.

I confess: I was one of these people!

This is why I was so excited when I discovered these highly effective sensory meditations. They not only work—they also do not feel like work! It's super fun to concentrate on your five senses—and far simpler to do than the most popular mainstream meditations, which mostly promote trying to concentrate on your breath.

Let me tell you—concentrating on taste, sound, smell, touch, and sight can actually be very enjoyable to do. And for me, it was a must that my stress-reducing method should be doable in a stress-free way!

These sensory meditations are all fun and simple good stuff—plus they are hugely effective at stopping a moving train of negative thoughts from plowing through your happy day.

Best of all, the feeling of inner peace that these tools bring comes swiftly because you can use these tools for as little as two minutes. In fact, if you're a busy person, you will love how you can easily sneak these calming tools into your schedule. I still turn to these sensory meditations all the time when I'm on a work deadline or dealing with a surprise curveball challenge.

I'm excited to share these awesome sensory meditation tools with you so that you can learn to become a happier, more relaxed version of you. Let's get started!

xo

karen

Tip: If you want to read all the cool articles and scientific studies behind the tools in this book, visit www.notsalmon.com/instant-calm-endnotes. I'll also keep the links updated with any fascinating new findings!

Sight
meditations

If you can stare at a beautiful ocean view, then you can do sight meditations!

Why? Because staring out across the sea is an organic form of sight meditation that you unwittingly do, and so, accidentally, relax yourself.

There's actually a neuroscientific reason a beautiful water view can chill you out. When you are mesmerized by the sight of crashing waves, you become so absorbed by the ocean's beauty that you no longer notice the beastly things worrying you!

Basically, when you're spellbound by the sight of a gorgeous ocean, you're telling your brain, "Yo! Do *not* focus on pain and anxiety! Focus *here* on this beauty that's right smack in front of me."

I believe that one of the reasons we love beautiful artwork is because artwork also serves as a kind of sight meditation. You're so focused and entranced by the sight of a stunning painting or sculpture that you're able—for that moment—to forget about stressful things.

When you do a sight meditation, you're showing your brain that *you* are in charge of your thoughts—that *you* decide to focus on beauty, not pain—and that *you* are the boss of your cerebrum!

With all this in mind, get ready to be very bossy-pants with your cerebrum! Coming up, you'll find five fun sight meditations, which I've named "meDOTations" because you stare at a dot in the middle of a colorful image.

Bonus: If you can successfully "meDOTate" on the dot—and only the dot—you will be greeted by a very cool optical illusion.

In fact, the better you are at mastering your thoughts and focusing only on the dot—in a *one-pointed way*, as the Buddhists call this uninterrupted, single-minded focus—the better this bonus optical illusion reward will be for you.

How to Do All 5 MeDOTations

1 Open up to a double-page spread with the specific meDOTation you want to do. Hold this book far enough away from you that you can clearly see the image with the dot (on the left side of the page) without your neck feeling strained.

2 Rest your eyes upon the dot inside the image and—lightly—meDOTate on the dot. Don't stare in a way that feels uncomfortable.

3 For your first time meDOTating, stay fully and mindfully focused on the dot for at least thirty seconds. Thereafter, keep stretching the amount of time you MeDOTate until you reach two minutes.

4 After the assigned time has passed, move your gaze to the middle of the image on the right side of the page spread. Blink your eyes a few times and enjoy the bonus optical illusion reward—as well as a nice, relaxing, feeling of calm. Sigh. . . .

Sunnier Mood-itation

Stay calm in any storm by focusing on the dot in the rainbow—and then staring off into the clouds.

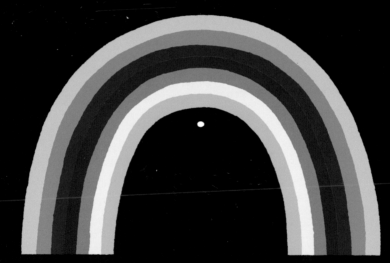

Love Is a Super (Calming) Power

Stay relaxed when feeling anger and resentment by focusing on the heart-shaped dot in "love"—and then on your new name tag.

HELLO

my name is

Aim for the Moon and Feel Like a Star

Stay calm and confident while seeking a goal by staring at the freckle dot—then the moon—and knowing the skies are no limit for you!

Keep Calm and Ommm Instead of NomNomNom

Stay calm and balanced so you don't stress-eat by staring at the dot inside the beautiful flower—then at the plate.

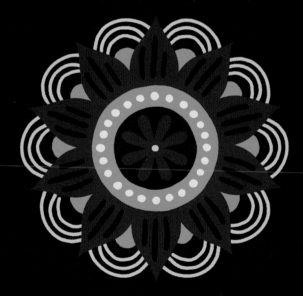

The Art of Happier Thoughts

Stay relaxed and positive during a challenge by staring at the dot in the art and reminding yourself that you have the power to reframe what happens to you as an opportunity for growth—then look at the blank space inside the frame and know better things are coming.

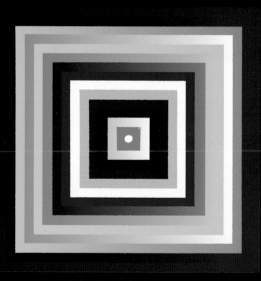

Smell
meditations

WARNING: The following pages might be the smelliest pages you've ever read!

Chances are you've done a smell meditation to calm yourself—without knowing you were doing one. For example, maybe you've walked into a bakery and inhaled the smell of freshly baked bread. Immediately, you felt a sense of inner peace—as well as a sense of "I want a piece!" (Mmmm . . . fresh-baked bread!)

Fact: The smell center of our brain is located in brain "real estate" right near the memory center. For this reason, neuroscientists have linked our earliest memories not to things we saw, but things we smelled.

Tip: Make sure you store your essential oil in a cool, dark place with the cap on tightly—to protect its yummy essence!

So if the smell of baby powder makes you feel more calm and smiley, it might be because it's triggering happy memories from your babyhood—when you felt pampered, supported, and fully taken care of.

Your sense of smell, also known as your olfactory response, is directly linked to your brain's emotional center—more so than any of your other senses. As a result, your sense of smell is not only the number one sense most connected to your memories—it is also the number one sense most connected to your emotions.

Meaning? If you really want to shift your emotions from frazzled to calm, then doing a smell meditation might be one of the most powerful holistic tools available for sending a flood of warm, fuzzy feelings throughout your body—and mind!

That is, if you choose the right scents! Read on. . . .

VANILLA HELPS YOUR BEAN

work better

MANY STUDIES, including one study by the Memorial Sloan Kettering Cancer Center in New York, report that the smell of vanilla can boost happiness and decrease stress.

The center actually tested the effects of five different fragrances on eighty-five patients undergoing an MRI scan. Of the five scents tested, vanilla was rated the number one most relaxing. In fact, patients exposed to the vanilla smell reported 63 percent less anxiety and claustrophobia than those not exposed.

Sloan Kettering was so impressed by vanilla's relaxing benefits that they now include the smell of vanilla as a standard part of their MRI scans!

How to do it

Inhale calm, exhale chaos: Get a bottle of vanilla essential oil. Hold it beneath your nose. Inhale and exhale for two minutes. Repeat the following: (Inhale) "I am stronger than my challenges." (Exhale) "My challenges are making me stronger."

extra credit

Double up the relaxing benefits of reading and create a homemade vanilla-scented bookmark! Put a few drops of vanilla essential oil on a bookmark. Leave it in a plastic bag overnight. Infuse your reading with extra calming benefits.

GRAPEFRUIT
COULD BE
RENAMED

greatfruit!

A STUDY on the power of grapefruit essential oils was done at the nurses' station at the James Cancer Hospital in Columbus, Ohio. These nurses were self-admitted frequent sufferers of work-related stress, compassion fatigue, and burnout. In this study, the nurses were instructed to regularly inhale grapefruit essential oil throughout their day.

The result? The nurses reported nursing themselves back to a better emotional state, with great improvements in their stress levels!

How to do it

Chakra it up: Get a bottle of grapefruit essential oil. If you have sensitive skin or just want to be extra-safe, dilute three to five drops in a teaspoon of carrier oil like coconut or almond oil. Dab some on the famous chakra point in the middle of your wrist. When stressed, smell your wrist. Repeat the following meditation: "I am open to feeling calm. I am open to receiving insights and guidance to help me with my situation." Keep the essential oil in your bag or briefcase. Reapply when needed.

extra credit

To lower work stress, add a few drops of grapefruit essential oil on a cotton pad. Place it next to your computer so that you inhale the calming scent as you work.

Fun fact: If you're a stress eater, you have double the reason to sniff the scent of grapefruit. A grapefruit's aroma is not only reported to lower stress—it's also reported to reduce food cravings, according to a study from Japan's Osaka University.

TURN PEPPERMINT INTO

content-mint

PEPPERMINT OIL is consistently recommended in aromatherapy to help relieve tension—and even headaches.

Practitioners and fans of peppermint oil report that it works as a healing and holistic aromatherapy treatment for tension headaches. Some researchers suggest that's because peppermint oil supports the flow of blood and opens the sinuses, both of which improve the flow of oxygen.

A study published in the journal *Nervenarzt* explored healing tension headaches by applying peppermint oil to the foreheads and temples of forty-one headache sufferers. The results? Peppermint oil was as effective as two extra-strength Tylenols!

WARNING: Pregnant women should avoid peppermint oil! Also, if you have any health issues, check with your doctor before trying it.

How to do it

Turn your temples into a temple of relaxation!
Get a bottle of peppermint essential oil. If you have
sensitive skin or just want to be extra-safe, dilute
three to five drops in a teaspoon of carrier oil like
coconut or almond oil. Massage a drop on your
temples or the back of your neck. Concentrate on
the scent for at least two minutes.

extra credit

Make a calming, hot minty soak for your feet by
adding a few drops of peppermint oil to a bowl or
bucket of water. Soak your tootsies! Bonus: Studies
show peppermint oil helps to kill bacteria.

ORANGE YOU GLAD YOU SMELLED

bergamot?

BERGAMOT IS a sweet and spicy scent, sourced from the peel of a citrus fruit known as *Citrus bergamia*. It smells like yummy oranges mixed with a pinch of feisty floral. Bergamot is actually the oil that gives Earl Grey tea its lovely aroma.

But it's more than just another pretty fragrance. It's a helpful mood balancer.

According to a review in *Frontiers in Pharmacology*, some studies indicate that bergamot essential oil can help reduce blood pressure and heart rate and lower anxiety.

A 2017 study described in *Phytotherapy Research* was performed on folks in the waiting room of a mental health treatment center. Researchers found that the aroma of bergamot greatly boosted these patients' positive feelings.

Why? According to a study published in the *Journal of the Korean Academy of Nursing*, the smell of a blend of oils that included bergamot—along with lavender and ylang-ylang—lowered serum cortisol levels, aka the body's stress hormone.

How to do it

Fire stress, fire up calm: Light a bergamot-scented candle. Let the scent infuse your environment. Spend two minutes inhaling the scent while thinking about an outcome you want. Fill in the blank in this meditation: "I'm at peace knowing I'll get to my goal of _____ in a way that is best for my long-term growth and fulfillment."

extra credit

Think about your wish coming true, and then blow out the candle before you leave your home. Trust the process.

LAVENDER IS YOUR BUD FOR
de-stressing

LAVENDER IS one of the oldest aromatherapy scents for relaxation. Persians, Greeks, and Romans would add it to their baths, believing it could help purify both mind and body. (The word *lavender* is derived from the Latin root *lavare*— "to wash.")

Modern studies agree with lavender's historically reported relaxing benefits. Lots of research shows that lavender helps to treat anxiety:

- According to a 2012 review in the *Natural Medicine Journal*, the scent of lavender works to calm anxiety because it influences the limbic system, the part of the brain that controls emotions.

- Another study in the *International Journal of Nursing Practices* reported that people who spritzed their clothes with a 3 percent lavender oil solution wound up reducing work-related stress.

- Bonus: A study in the *Journal of Alternative and Complementary Medicine* reported the scent of lavender helped to improve the memories of stressed-out people!

How to do it

Look stress in the face! Add a few drops of lavender oil to a bowl of hot water. Drape a towel over your head. Lean your face over the bowl. Inhale the relaxing lavender-scented steam for two minutes. Bonus: Your skin pores will thank you by giving you a glowing complexion!

extra credit

Keep a satchel of lavender in your underwear drawer as a morning mood calmer! Every morning when you get dressed, take a thirty-second "morning hit" of this scent to start your day off centered.

Sound
meditations

When you're anxious, your brain becomes a noisy place. Unfortunately, the most negative thoughts tend to speak up the loudest.

It's tough to lower the volume on this cranky chatter. But you can drown it out with sound meditations.

Chances are you've done a sound meditation—and not realized it—whenever you've gotten lost in the sound of your favorite music.

You know how you're more able to tune out negative thoughts when you're grooving to some good tunes? Well, that's because you're doing a sound meditation of sorts.

They say music has the power to soothe the savage beast. I've personally found that to be true. The right song has definitely soothed my inner savage beast.

As it turns out, the calming power of music has been backed by research. Lots of studies support that music has a relaxing effect on our minds and bodies. In fact, many people seek the comfort of music before, during, and after surgery, believing in its calming powers.

Researchers from Queen Mary University, Barts Health NHS Trust, and Brunel University found that patients who listened to music not only experienced more calm—they also wound up requesting less pain relievers.

Music has been used therapeutically for patients in operating rooms since 1914. Florence Nightingale has even been rumored to have enlisted music to help soothe and relax her patients.

In the same way sound meditations can distract patients from physical pain, they can distract you from emotional pain.

Thankfully, music is not the only "sound advice" I'm recommending! Read on. . . .

OM *sweet* OM

CHANCES ARE you've heard of the famous "om" meditation—where monks chant "ommmmmm" to reach a state of inner peace.

Maybe you've chanted "ommmm" in a yoga class and felt more grounded.

As it turns out, there's a scientific reason why chanting "om" relaxes you. This sound creates a vibration in your throat—in particular, "a vagus nerve stimulation through its auricular branches."

I know I just sounded really scientifically smart right now.

Full confession: Those words are grabbed from a report published in the *International Journal of Yoga* on people who chanted "om" versus people who just said the sound "sssss."

The results? Chanting "om" creates a beneficial vibration that sends a "cue" to your brain to relax. In contrast, people who simply said "sssss" did not get this same helpful signal to the brain to relax.

How to do it

Chants encounter: Chant "ommmm" as if that O and those Ms are three to four syllables long— and as if you're saying "aum." Feel the vibration fully in your throat and chest. Hold each "om" for about ten to fifteen seconds—and repeat ten in a row. Ooooooooooommmmmmmmmm. . . .

extra credit

If you put a little "om" into "insomnia," you could fall asleep a little more easily. Basically, if you're having trouble falling asleep because you're feeling sad and worried about your life, try a little "om therapy" while lying in bed with your eyes closed. Chanting "om" is reported to alleviate depression, according to an eight-week study by the Samarya Center for Integrated Movement Therapy and Ashtanga Yoga.

TAKE A
forest bath

IF YOU WANT to feel more calm—you can go jump in a lake! Or go take a hike!

I know these things sound like insults—but I'm saying them with loving intentions. I want you to immerse yourself in the sounds of nature as a therapeutic sound meditation.

This tool is research-backed by scientists in Japan. They found that listening to nature sounds is stress reducing.

They call it *shinrin-yoku*, which means "forest bath."

Japanese researchers found that even just a tiny twenty-minute forest bath could change the blood flow in the cerebellum such that an individual experiences relaxation.

Similarly, studies in the United States consistently show that listening to sounds of nature helps folks to relax. A research team at the University of Florida reported that listening to sounds of ocean waves worked even better than simple silence or music by Mozart. In fact, those who listened to ocean waves had much lower levels of muscle tension, heart rate, and stress. Plus these relaxing results occurred within a speedy few minutes.

Forest bathing does not simply work because you're doing lots of walking. Researchers at the Nippon Medical School compared walking in the city to taking a forest walk. The result? Walking in the forest created a far greater reduction in blood pressure and certain stress hormones. Meaning? It's the forest environment that is truly responsible for lowering anxiety.

How to do it

The giving tree: The first choice would be to get away to a forest (or an ocean) for a few minutes. But that can be kind of expensive and complicated to do in the middle of the day! Luckily, you can visit my site (www.notsalmon.com/free-stuff) for a range of curated forest sounds and ocean sounds that you can listen to for two minutes. Close your eyes and focus on letting the sounds transport you to that calming environment.

extra credit

As you listen to forest sounds, you might want to smell cedar oil or cedar chips for a full 3-D forest environment effect! Scientists believe the scent of cedar tree compounds is part of the reason forest bathing helps to reduce blood pressure.

GIVE YOURSELF
tlc
WITH NLP

FEELING STRESSED? Try a neurolinguistic programming–enhanced mantra!

A mantra is a sacred utterance—either a word or a group of words with positive associations—that you say out loud.

Mantras make a very relaxing sound meditation, and that's a research-backed opinion. A study in *Brain and Behavior* reported that repeating a single-word mantra, even without a spiritual context or other practices typical of meditation, had a definite calming effect.

I believe mantras work because they do double duty as a neurolinguistic programming (NLP) tool. NLP is a therapy built on the belief that using positive and self-loving language can influence your subconscious mind.

How to do it

Some NLP TLC to do ASAP: Repeat the phrase "Everything always works out for me." For best results, say it while looking in the mirror at yourself. Vary how you say it so these words don't become "white noise." Say it slowly, then quickly, then softly, then loudly. Repeat for two minutes.

extra credit

Repeat the word *calm*—but pronounce it "calmmmmm." Doing this for two minutes, you'll get the NLP benefits from the positive word *calm*—plus you'll cash in on the vibrational benefits of chanting "ommmmm."

DO SOME
weightless
TRAINING

UK-BASED Mindlab International reports that music truly helps people to release stress. In particular, the song "Weightless" by Marconi Union decreased anxiety by 65 percent and reduced physiological resting rates (such as blood pressure) by as much as 35 percent. Wowzer!

The study: Subjects were connected to sensors that measured brain activity and physiological states, like heart rate, blood pressure, and breathing. Next, they were given difficult, stress-inducing puzzles to solve while they listened to different songs.

According to the study director, Dr. David Lewis-Hodgson, all the relaxing songs helped to some degree—but "Weightless" wound up bringing about the greatest sense of relaxation.

Why? Therapists helped design this song to calm people! It has specific harmonies and rhythms to control heart rate, reduce blood pressure, and lower levels of cortisol.

How to do it

Weight lifting from your heart and mind:
Download the song "Weightless" or find the music video for it online—or simply queue up some of your favorite calming classical music. After you choose your music, find a comfortable place to sit or lie down. Play the song while breathing deeply for a minimum of two minutes either while watching the soothing video images or with your eyes closed.

extra credit

If classical music is more your thing, listen up! Consistently, studies recommend listening to classical music as a calming techique, because it's reported to slow down the pulse and heart rate.

WARNING: "Weightless" was so effective at making people more calm—and even drowsy—that the study director advises people against driving while listening to this song!

SELECTIVE

listening

WE LIVE in a noisy world with lots of honking traffic, blaring technology, barking dogs, and shouting people! All of this audio chaos creates inner chaos—which increases stress.

Consistently, studies report that too much noise can have a negative effect on our heart rate, ability to focus, mood—and even our hormones.

"Sound affects the human body deeply," says sound expert and the Sound Agency founder Julian Treasure in *Shape*. "We experience it faster than any other sense, and our ears are working even when we're asleep."

Thankfully, I have a simple tool to help you take back control over the loud noises around you— and the loud negative chatter blaring inside your head.

Simply do some selective listening, where you mindfully select three specific sounds to focus on.

How to do it

Set yourself "three" from stress: Close your eyes so that you're forced to pay close attention to the sounds around you. Quiet your mind and listen for three distinct sounds. What can you hear around you?

- The sound of birds chirping?
- The sound of a clock?
- The sound of a distant car?

Concentrate on listening to these three things for two minutes. Alternate between these sounds—so you are the one orchestrating the sounds you allow into your head. Soon you will be able to stop your busy, chattering-monkey mind from doing its stressful monkey business!

extra credit

Lower the volume on your workout. According to a study by Massachusetts Eye and Ear, the average spin class exposes you to about nine times more noise in forty-five minutes than what's normally recommended over eight hours. This noise overload can stress you out—and damage your hearing. Solution? Wear earplugs in workout classes and stay far from the speakers.

Touch
meditations

I want to help you feel less anxiety—by feeling more things with your hands!

Yes! I'm gonna help you to be less touchy . . . by giving you a range of things to touch. There are a variety of fun (and G-rated) touch meditations that have you reaching out and touching soft stuff, wet stuff, scratchy stuff, and grassy stuff.

Chances are that you've done a touch meditation before—without realizing it.

When you were a kid, you probably had a teddy bear or some favorite stuffed animal toy. One of the reasons you loved your stuffed animal (other than the fact that it was so gosh darn adorable) was because it was so gosh darn soft. Every time you hugged your stuffed animal, you became mesmerized by its comforting softness.

You were unwittingly doing a touch meditation. The feel of its cozy fur wound up distracting you from whatever was making you sad or scared. Eventually, the more you hugged your soft and cuddly stuffed animal, the more comfort you felt.

In this way, your stuffed animal became an anchoring tool. Simply touching it lightly made you feel incredibly safe and secure.

Coming up are a few recommended tactile treats to help you relax during stressful times. If you regularly use these touch meditations, you'll have a powerful arsenal—literally!—at your fingertips.

earthing

TO FEEL CALMER DOWN TO YOUR NAKED TOES

HERE'S A RELAXATION remedy that dates back thousands of years. It's called *earthing*. You simply walk barefoot on the earth.

It might sound hippie-dippie, but earthing is actually a science-backed stress management tool.

When you *ground* a piece of electrical equipment, you connect it to the ground so that any excess electrical charge can run off in a harmless way. This same theory is said to apply to walking on the earth with your bare feet. You are basically earthing your body in the same way you are grounding electrical equipment. By connecting to the earth, you allow negatively charged electrons to flow into your body—plus you allow your excess positively charged particles to run off into the ground . . . thereby returning your body to optimum health.

Top benefits for earthing include

- fighting inflammation by reducing free radicals, which are positively charged.

- improving sleep.

- lowering stress.

- promoting calmness and a positive mood.

Tip: Remove your shoes when you get home and walk barefoot. It will stimulate relaxing acupressure points on your feet, plus cut down on trailing in toxins and bacteria from your shoes!

How to do it

Calm your soul via your soles: Take two minutes to walk barefoot atop grass or sand or anywhere your feet will come in direct contact with the ground. Concentrate on the feel of the texture beneath your feet. (If you're at home, mindfully walk barefoot on your wooden, tiled, or carpeted floor. You might not technically be earthing, but you can still stimulate those acupressure points while having a relaxing touch meditation—this is especially enjoyable if you have lots of cozy shag carpeting!)

extra credit

If you're gonna spend time earthing, treat yourself to a nice pedicure so that you can proudly flaunt your tootsies. Plus a pedicure makes a wonderfully relaxing touch meditation!

doodle
TO RELAX
YOUR NOODLE

REMEMBER WHEN you were in school and loved to doodle repeated patterns and swirly images in your notebooks?

Well, you were accidentally doing a self-soothing, relaxation exercise—a form of art therapy. It's believed that the repetition and rhythmic motions of doodling wind up triggering the *relaxation response*, which is the antidote to the famous stressful *fight-or-flight response*.

Researchers call doodling by the fancy name *spontaneous drawing* and consistently report that it reduces cortisol, the stress hormone, thereby helping people to feel calmer and happier.

One study from Drexel University examined the brains of doodlers, who were asked to draw free-form and also to color in geometric patterns. Researchers found this doodling stuff wound up stimulating more blood flow to the prefrontal cortex—the part of the brain famously known as the "reward center"!

Meaning? Doodling triggers the same brain area as chocolate, laughing, and dancing.

Sunni Brown also spoke about the many benefits of doodling in her viral TED talk. In particular, she explained how doodling not only calms nerves but also helps support memory, comprehension, and problem-solving abilities. Brown explained how doodling keeps the doodler fully present in the moment—and that's a very calming place to be!

How to do it

Draw out the best in you: Get a blank journal or grab some paper. For two to five minutes, scribble a series of repetitive strokes: straight lines, curves, dots, swirls, and shapes.

extra credit

You can give your doodles to a therapist to analyze. It may help you deal with your stress in a deeper way. Dr. Robert Burns, the former director of the Institute for Human Development at the University of Seattle, analyzes the doodles of his patients, believing these scribbles give a sneak peek at one's unconscious mind.

GIVE YOURSELF A

hand

THIS TOUCH-CONCENTRATION meditation is very handy.

Literally very handy. You practice hand reflexology by touching yourself on the hand at specific acupressure points.

In a 2017 hand reflexology study published in *Complementary Therapies in Clinical Practice*, patients who were to undergo coronary angiography were divided into two groups. Group 1 was given hand reflexology. Group 2 got nada. The people who received this simple hand massage wound up feeling a lot less anxiety.

A 2011 study at the University of Portsmouth reported how hand reflexology helps to treat stress-related headaches. According to this six-month study, the people who did these hand massages received the following benefits:

- 55 percent experienced reduced symptoms.

- 23 percent stopped having headaches completely.

- 19 percent were able to stop taking headache medication.

WARNING: Pregnant women should avoid acupressure because certain pressure points can induce contractions! Also, if you have any health issues, check with your doctor before trying acupressure.

How to do it

Palm reading: Next time you're feeling anxious, reach out and feel an acupressure point!

- Feeling overwhelmed? Gently massage your HT7 point for one minute on each hand. This acupressure point can be found right below your wrist crease, where your outer hand is.

- Got a stress headache? Gently massage—and even pinch—your fleshy LI4 point for one minute on each hand.

extra credit

Memorial Sloan Kettering Cancer Center recommends doing hand acupressure to promote blood circulation and alleviate physical pain throughout your body.

PET A
pet

FEELING STRESSED? Simply reach out and pet a pet.

According to doctors at Johns Hopkins, petting an animal can increase levels of the stress-reducing hormone oxytocin and decrease production of the stress hormone cortisol.

Actually, I've personally done my own research on this petting-a-pet tool with our Havanese dog Fluffy—and I can tell you that petting this cutie-pie feels good (to the touch) *and* makes me feel good.

I love his soft fur. I can easily get lost in it and forget about whatever was on my mind.

How to do it

The cuddle cure: Find a dog, cat, or furry pet of some kind to cuddle up with. If you don't have a pet, see if you can borrow someone else's. They might let you—if you offer to dog-walk or cat-sit for free! Or simply visit a dog park or cat café and make some new furry friends.

Bonus: If you're allergic to furry creatures—or simply a huge fan of that furry feeling—get yourself a faux fur blanket.

extra credit

Find someone you trust and give them a nice, long hug. Yep—a study from the University of North Carolina showed that hugging can lower blood pressure and boost oxytocin!

SHOWER
POWER
meditation

TAKE A SHOWER and multitask by washing away your stress and anxiety. Concentrate on the feel of the water on your skin.

There's actually a fancy scientific term for the proven feel-good joy a shower brings: *hydrotherapy*. Translation? It's the curative use of water to help with health, pain, and relaxation.

Hot-off-the-press info: Researchers at the Swedish University of Agricultural Sciences linked the elements of hot showers to boosts in oxytocin levels and reduced anxiety.

Some very cool info: According to researchers at the Virginia Commonwealth University School of Medicine, a cold shower is both invigorating and mood boosting. Why? The shock of cold activates beta-endorphins (the molecules famed for creating a sense of well-being) and noradrenaline in the brain—both of which put you in a better mood. (That second one is actually something found in many antidepressants.)

No matter the temperature you pick, simply immersing yourself in water is reported to increase production of beta-endorphins.

How to do it

Wash away your negativity: Step into the shower. Become aware of the water's temperature—its balance of hot versus cold. Squeeze out some body wash and feel its soft sudsiness on your skin. Grab a loofah and feel its scratchy surface on your skin. After you've done this for a few minutes, take some time to envision the power of the shower water washing away your negative thoughts! Whoosh! Envision fear, regret, and anger soaping off you and swirling down the drain.

extra credit

Sing in the shower. Researchers at the University of East Anglia report that singing for fun (without the pressure of performing) helps relieve both anxiety and depression.

Fun fact: Thomas Jefferson enjoyed a freezing cold foot bath every morning for sixty years, believing it improved his health.

Taste
meditations

I want to start this section by sharing two funny oxymorons:

- A stand is something you sit in.
- Having a coffee break helps me feel more calm.

Let's consider the latter. Coffee contains caffeine. Coffee should not help me become more calm. But it relaxes me because I'm doing an accidental taste meditation.

When I'm having a really good cup of coffee, I'm fully in the moment. I'm not worrying about the past or the future. I'm just enjoying my time with my yummy BFF—coffee.

I don't know if you feel the same way about coffee as I do. But I'm guessing you've gotten lost in the yummy flavor of something . . . and thereby done an accidental taste meditation too.

Coming up, I'm going to give you some tools to do an accidental taste meditation—on purpose, which I guess is another oxymoron.

That—and "airplane food."

Really? The airlines call that food?

No worries—I'm not going to ask you to do a taste meditation with airplane food.

THROW A
TEA PARTY
FOR YOUR
mind

I'M NOT the first to recommend tea as a taste meditation. The Japanese have been recommending tea as an opportunity for meditation for eons—in the form of tea ceremonies.

The Japanese tea ceremony is famously summed up by the Zen phrase *ichi-go ichi-e*, which means "one time, one meeting."

This phrase is meant to remind us that there's beauty and uniqueness to be found in the present moment—and that this moment will never come again—so you should give it your complete awareness and appreciation.

I'm excited to help you maintain an *ichi-go ichi-e* mind-set for this taste meditation.

I recommend the following three teas, which doubly relax you because of their ingredients:

- CHAMOMILE: Known to reduce stress and anxiety and to treat insomnia.

- LEMON BALM: Reported to reduce the stress hormone cortisol and allow you to relax without drowsiness.

- GREEN: Contains polyphenol, which helps combat anxiety. Although it contains caffeine, it's said to be adaptogenic, meaning that it keeps your mind alert while calming you.

How to do it

Sip your way to sereni-tea: Select a relaxing tea. Make your tea in mindfulness. Admire the color. Become aware of the journey the tea took from being a leaf on a tree or shrub to your taste meditation. Give thanks.

Drink your tea with mindfulness—with very small sips. Savor the flavor. Do not allow thoughts to wander outside the taste of the tea. End with gratitude. Thank the tea for giving you this calming break.

extra credit

You can use tea bags as excellent aromatherapy sachets for drawers and closets.

DARK CHOCOLATE HAS A

bright side

THIS RELAXATION homework assignment is all about chocolate. Lucky you!

I'm assigning you the task of eating dark chocolate for a few reasons:

- It's blessed with a huge attention-hogging yummy taste, which, when focused on, can distract you from your worries.

- It's therapeutically blessed (if 70 percent cacao or more)—shown by research to help reduce stress levels in the brain—true story.

- Dark chocolate contains serotonin, endorphin, and dopamine, which are great hormones for lowering stress levels.

According to an interesting chocolate study in the *Journal of Proteome Research*, some super-lucky study subjects were asked to eat one and a half ounces of dark chocolate a day for two weeks. By the end of this time period, they were shown to have greatly reduced levels of stress hormones!

How to do it

Melt away stress: Take a nice one-and-a-half ounce chunk of dark chocolate. Allow it to melt in your mouth . . . slowly. Resist chewing—really savor the flavor. Stop thinking about all the things wrong with your life. Remain focused only on all the things right about dark chocolate!

extra credit

Doing a taste meditation is all about savoring the flavor—not binge-eating, which is the opposite of a taste meditation. When you binge-eat, you basically do not taste the food. You inhale it. Be sure to savor the flavor of the chocolate—and be sure to do this taste meditation only once a day, not one hundred times a day!

BANANAS HELP YOU NOT GO
bananas

I THINK the expression "to go bananas" is another oxymoron because bananas actually can help stop you from going bananas!

Bananas are a recommended food for relaxing. They are a natural beta blocker. Meaning? They block adrenaline from binding to beta receptors, which then lowers blood pressure and pulse rate.

Plus bananas are high in potassium, which also helps regulate blood pressure, so bananas offer a nice, soothing relief for the brain and body. In fact, low levels of potassium are reported to contribute to stress and anxiety.

Unfortunately, anxiety itself can cause the level of the stress hormone adrenaline in your body to increase, which then causes your cells to use up lots of potassium—which then lowers your potassium levels.

Meaning? If you're particularly stressed-out, you may be low on potassium, so it's extra important to gobble up foods that are rich in potassium.

How to do it

A highly "a-peeling" meditation: Unpeel a banana. Put it in freezer-safe wrapping—and wait for it to freeze. Enjoy the banana as a frozen banana pop so that you eat it more slowly and really lose yourself in its yumminess. For the entire time you're slooooowwwwly enjoying your banana pop, make sure that whenever you think a thought that drives you bananas—you only think about that yummy banana flavor instead.

extra credit

Some speakers, performers, and musicians say they eat one banana about thirty minutes before they go on stage to help relieve stage fright. You can try the same before a test or presentation.

tongue
TWISTER
UPPERS

GET READY to take your taste buds on a flavor-tripping ride—thanks to "miracle fruit," also known as *Synsepalum dulcificum* and commonly available as miracle fruit tablets.

A miracle fruit tablet is a taste-altering lozenge that magically changes the taste of sour, spicy, and savory foods into a surprisingly sweet taste.

I've tried it—and witnessed it transforming the taste of tangy lemon slices and spicy chili peppers into the flavor of child-friendly, sugary-sweet candies. Plus it intensifies the taste of strawberries.

How? Miracle fruit contains *miraculin*, a protein that alters your tongue's taste buds for fifteen minutes to two hours. The berries have even been used to help people with chemotherapy-related taste disturbances enjoy their food more—and people with diabetes to eat less sugar-laden foods. And of course, if you cut back on sugar, you'll be calmer! Best of all, the berries help to distract your busy, chattering-monkey mind, because you'll be so singularly focused on the magical transformative effect they have on your taste buds.

How to do it

Taste switcheroo: Dissolve a miracle fruit tablet under your tongue. Taste one of the following foods:

- Lemons (taste like cotton candy)
- Chili peppers (taste innocently sweet)
- Cream cheese (tastes like cheesecake)
- Strawberries (taste like they've been dipped in sugar)

For two minutes, concentrate on the fascinating new flavor your food now has, focusing on how the flavor has switched to sweet—while you think or say this meditation: "Just as I can change this food's taste into something sweet, I can change pain into gain and problems into solutions."

extra credit

Eliminating one of our senses can make it easier to concentrate on another sense! Try doing this exercise blindfolded to achieve an even stronger laser-focus.

WARNING: Be careful tasting acidic and spicy foods. They'll taste sweet but are harsh on your stomach. Eat in moderation.

HONEY,
JUST
relax!

NEXT TIME you're feeling stressed, you might want to spend some time with your honey—a bottle of local organic honey, that is.

I'm recommending honey for two reasons:

- Honey offers a positively delicious distraction from your bad mood.
- Honey scientifically helps to reduce anxiety and nerves.

As you might already know, honey contains the relaxation-inducing amino acid tryptophan. Spanish researchers at the University of Extremadura reported that foods rich in tryptophan lessened anxiety—and even helped people fall asleep.

Plus, unlike processed sugars, eating honey raises your blood sugar level only slightly. This small rise of insulin causes the tryptophan to enter your brain slowly and get converted into serotonin. And in darkness, serotonin is converted into melatonin, a well-known cure for sleeping disorders.

How to do it

Use this honeycomb tool—and stop pulling out your hair: Cut a small square out of a piece of fresh honeycomb. (If you can't find honeycomb at your local market or beehive, substitute a natural honey lozenge.) Suck the honey out of the honeycomb, allowing it to dissolve as slowly as possible in your mouth. Become fully aware of its texture as well as its sweetness. Think only sweet thoughts for the time the honey is dissolving in your mouth.

extra credit

When you feel like you've reached the last straw, reach for a honey-filled straw!

Ten Speed Press and the Ten Speed Press colophon are registered
trademarks of Penguin Random House LLC.

Some of the material in this book was originally published in somewhat
different form as part of "The Anxiety Cure" video course by Karen
Salmansohn on NotSalmon.com.

Author photo copyright © Laura DeSantis-Olsson

Library of Congress Cataloging-in-Publication Data
Names: Salmansohn, Karen, author.
Title: Instant calm : 2-minute meditations to create a lifetime of happy /
    Karen Salmansohn.
Description: New York : Ten Speed Press, 2019.
Identifiers: LCCN 2019001538| ISBN 9780399582899 (hardback) |
    ISBN 9780399582905 (eISBN)
Subjects: LCSH: Mindfulness (Psychology) | Meditation. | Stress
    management. |
    BISAC: SELF-HELP / Meditations. | SELF-HELP / Motivational &
    Inspirational. | BODY, MIND & SPIRIT / Meditation.
Classification: LCC BF637.M56 S25 2019 | DDC 158.1/28—dc23 LC
    record available at https://lccn.loc.gov/2019001538

Hardcover ISBN: 978-0-399-58289-9
eBook ISBN: 978-0-399-58290-5

Printed in China

Design by Lisa Schneller Bieser

10 9 8 7 6 5 4 3 2 1

First Edition